Mom

I Want to Hear
About Your

Life

Published by Midsummer Bloom Books

First Edition: February 2025
Printed in the United States of America

Contents

Your Story Starts Here

Remember those kitchen talks, Mom? The ones where you'd start telling us about your childhood while making Sunday dinner, and somehow we'd all end up sitting at the table long after the food was gone? Or those random car rides when you'd suddenly mention your first apartment or that terrible boss you had before we were born? We always wanted to hear more.

That's really what this book is about. Because in between the school pickups, the holiday planning, and making sure everyone had clean socks, there's this whole other life you've lived that we only get in bits and pieces. Not the stuff that shows up in family photos, but the real stuff – like how you felt on your first day of school, that classmate who became a lifelong friend, or what actually went through your mind when you met Dad.

Each page here is just a starting point. A little nudge to recall the girl who kept a diary under her mattress, or the teenager who saved babysitting money for concert tickets. The young woman figuring out her path when nothing was certain. Those stories aren't just your history – they're the beginning of ours too.

No need to rush through these pages. Maybe something will come to mind while you're watering plants, or during those quiet evening moments when the house finally settles down.

The thing is, Mom, when you share your stories – even the messy, complicated ones – you're giving us something we can't find anywhere else. They're like finding missing puzzle pieces to understanding not just you, but parts of ourselves too.

So grab a comfortable spot and that throw blanket you love. Maybe even that chocolate you hide from everyone else.

Your stories matter, Mom. And we've been waiting to hear them.

How to Use This Book

Throughout this book, you'll find thought-starters and memory prompts beneath each question. These are simply suggestions to spark ideas and memories - feel free to use them as inspiration or take your story in completely different directions. There are no right or wrong ways to share your life stories here. Just enjoy looking back on the path that led you here.

Before you were "Mom," you were you—

Dreams in starlight, courage in quiet moments,

Laughter with friends, tears no one saw.

These aren't footnotes to your story;

They're the pages that taught you to love us

In all the ways only you can.

1

Blossoming Beginnings

Time ripples like gentle waves, carrying forward the stories of those who shaped you. Your first breaths, first smiles, and the arms that welcomed you into this world.

First Light of Day

Every life begins with a story, one carefully preserved in the hearts of those who welcomed us. The details of your arrival create the opening chapter of your unique journey.

Share the story of how you entered this world, as it was told to you. What details about your birth day did your parents love sharing with you?

• Family setting

• Special moment

Tell us about the world you were born into - what was happening in your family's life?

• Time period

• Family story

Tell us about the person who first held you and what they often said about that moment.

• First embrace

• Their words

Ancestral Roots

Paint a picture of the lands our family came from - the villages, cities, or countries that shaped who we became. The histories carried in our blood...

What language or words from our ancestors still echo in our family today?

- The language

- Daily usage

Tell us about a place from your family's past that you feel deeply connected to.

- First stories

- Deep connection

What's a family story about 'the old country' that shaped who we are?

- Distant tale

- Family values

Family Tree Branches

Weave together the stories of the aunts, uncles, and cousins who colored your childhood world. Those familiar faces at family gatherings...

Tell us about a favorite aunt or uncle who brought something special to your childhood.

• Unique bond

• Special times

What was special about visiting your grandparents' home with all the cousins?

• House feeling

• Special treats

Share a family character whose personality brought color to family gatherings.

• Unique spirit

• Best stories

The Old Family Home

Within those familiar walls lived countless moments that shaped your world. Each room held its own melody – footsteps on floors, laughter in hallways, whispers at bedtime.

Describe the house where your story began – the stairs, the familiar scents, the way sunlight fell through those windows...

Which scenes from your childhood home still feel alive today? Paint us a picture of:

• The front entrance

• Family gathering spots

Tell us about your favorite corner or spot in your childhood home.

• Special place

• Secret comfort

What sounds and scents from your childhood home still live in your memory?

• Daily music

• Home fragrance

Kitchen Aromas

Some memories live in scents - bread rising in the oven, Sunday dinners simmering, holiday spices dancing in the air. These fragrances tell stories of comfort, love, and belonging.

Remember those moments in the family kitchen - the recipes being crafted, the warmth of the oven, the dishes that meant "home"...

Share a kitchen memory that takes you back to your childhood home.

• Cooking sounds

• Warm feeling

Share a kitchen disaster story that became a family legend.

• Funny moment

• Good laugh

What's a comfort food that reminds you of someone special?

• How it tastes

• Who made it

Family Traditions

Like delicate threads woven through time, our traditions bind us to-gether. Each ritual carries meaning that transcends the ordinary mo-ments of life.

Share the beautiful customs that marked our days - the small rituals and grand celebrations that made our family unique...

Tell us about a special tradition that brings back your happiest child-hood memories.

• What did you do together?

• Why special?

Share how your family celebrated holidays in ways that made them unique.

• Special touch

• Family style

What everyday rituals made your childhood home feel special?

• Daily magic

• Special moments

Grandmother's Lullabies

In the gentle moments between day and dreams, grandmother's voice would weave melodies that carried love in every note. These songs became the soundtrack of security and tenderness.

Remember the gentle songs that filled your earliest days - the soft melodies and the way your mother's voice would soothe your world to sleep...

What lullabies did your mother sing most often?

• Songs remembered

• When and how she sang them

Which special song always calmed you down?

• Comfort song

• The memories it brings back

Share a bedtime ritual that made you feel safe and loved.

• Gentle touch

• Soft words

Grandfather's Strong Hands

"A father's hands reflect his heart - rough from work, gentle from love." - Unknown

Recall those moments with your father - his presence in your early world, the way he guided you, the strength and safety you felt in his company...

Tell us about a special lesson or skill your father taught you.

• Shared moments

• Life wisdom

Share a memory that shows your father's unique way of showing love.

• His special ways

• Love language

What adventure or activity was special between you and your father?

• Together time

• Shared joy

The Family Table

Paint a picture of those shared meals - the gathering of familiar faces, the conversations that flowed, the special dishes that brought everyone together...

Tell us about dinner time rituals from your childhood home.

• Mealtime habits

• Table rules

What conversations or stories do you remember from family meals?

• Table talk

• Memory gems

What made Sunday dinners or holiday meals extra special?

• Special touch

• Family flavor

Sibling Stories

"Sisters and brothers are the truest, purest forms of love, friendship, and support." – *Marian Wright Edelman*

Share the early chapters of life with your brothers and sisters – the adventures and the unspoken bonds that grew stronger with time...

Tell us the story behind each sibling's name and nickname.

• Name roots

• Their nicknames

What games or activities were special between you and your siblings?

• Play time

• Why special?

What funny habits or quirks do you remember about each sibling?

• Unique behaviors

• The memories that make you smile

Neighborhood Tales

Our street was more than addresses and houses; it was a world of adventures waiting to unfold. Every neighbor held stories that shaped our community.

Describe the world beyond your doorstep - the neighbors who became like family, the streets where your childhood played out...

Tell us about the neighbors who became like extended family.

• Door open

• Life share

Share about the neighborhood gathering spots where children played.

• Where kids met to play

• Favorite outdoor spots

Tell us about neighborhood traditions or celebrations you remember.

• Special events

• How the community celebrated

2

The Girl in the Mirror

Little feet in oversized shoes, playing dress-up with dreams. Those precious early years when the world was new and every day brought wonder.

Morning Rituals

Each day began with its own rhythm - the soft morning light, familiar sounds floating through the house, the comforting sequence of getting ready.

What was the gentle rhythm of your mornings like? Think about the sounds, smells, and routines that started each day of your young life.

Tell us about the first sounds and smells that would wake you up.

• Wake calls

• Day start

Tell us about breakfast traditions in your childhood home.

• Table time

• Food love

What morning tasks or chores were part of your routine?

• Help hands

• Must dos

Dress-Up Dreams

"Playing dress-up begins at age five and never truly ends." - Kate Spade

Share about that special party dress, those shiny shoes, or the costume that made you feel magical. Which outfits held the dearest memories?

Tell us about your favorite dress or outfit from childhood.

• Special piece

• How it made you feel

Share about playing dress-up with family clothes or accessories.

• Mom's gems

• Role play

What were your favorite dress-up characters or roles?

• Characters you loved to be

• Your make-believe stories

Dollhouse Days

Within those miniature rooms lived stories of endless possibility. Each tiny piece represented a world where I could create and understand life in my own special way.

Remember your favorite childhood companions - the dolls, stuffed animals, and toys that were more than just playthings...

Tell us about your favorite doll or stuffed friend.

• Its name

• Its story

Tell us about how you cared for and 'fixed' your special toys.

• Care show

• Fix ways

Tell us about sharing or playing dolls with friends or siblings.

• Games you played together

• Stories you created

Backyard Adventures

Our yard was an endless frontier – trees became ships, flowers turned into fairy homes. Nature provided the perfect playground for discovery.

What mysteries and adventures awaited in your backyard? The trees you climbed, the hideouts you built, the treasures you discovered...

Tell us about the garden games and adventures you created.

· Games you invented

· Backyard adventures

What wildlife encounters made your backyard magical?

· Bird friends

· Bug finds

Tell us about backyard projects or forts you built.

· How you built your hideouts

· Special outdoor spaces

Hidden Corners

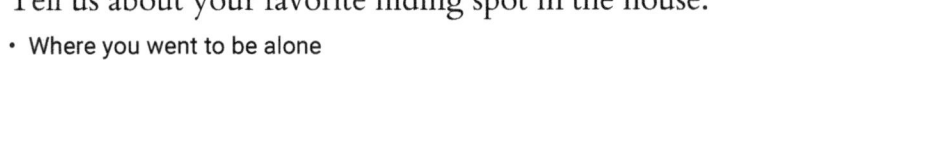

Every house holds secret spaces - the quiet nook behind the stairs, the window seat perfect for reading, the special spot where dreams feel closest at hand.

Tell me about your secret spots - behind the curtains, under the stairs, or in that quiet nook where you would escape to dream...

Tell us about your favorite hiding spot in the house.

- Where you went to be alone

- Why your favorite

Share about the window spots where you watched the world.

- Favorite window view

- What you liked to watch

Tell us about secret storage spots for treasures.

- Where you kept special things

- Your collections

Neighborhood Friends

"A friend is one of the nicest things you can have and one of the best things you can be." – *Winnie the Pooh*

Who were the familiar faces that shared your childhood adventures? The doorbell rings and laughter echoing down the street...

Tell us about meeting your first best friend.

• First hello

• Bond start

What adventures or mischief did you create together?

• Fun find

• Time wild

What friend moments taught you about loyalty and trust?

• Heart test

• Growth share

Rainy Day Fun

When clouds gathered outside, creativity flourished within. Board games and indoor picnics turned ordinary spaces into extraordinary adventures.

What magic did you create indoors when rain tapped on windows? The games and cozy moments that brightened grey days...

What indoor games became rainy day favorites?

• Games played

• Fun created

How did you transform indoor spaces creatively?

• Space changed

• Area decorated

Which indoor crafts kept you busy?

• Crafts made

• Projects done

Growing Girl's Room

My room was more than four walls – it was my creative space, my corner of the world. Each poster and treasured item told a story of who I was becoming.

Describe your childhood sanctuary – the decorations and the treasures on display...

Tell us about decorating your room for the first time.

• Wall art

• Color choice

What treasured items lived on your shelves?

• Things you displayed

• Items you were proud of

Tell us about how your room changed as you grew.

• How you decorated

• Style shift

Birthday Celebrations

Each birthday marked not just another year, but a celebration of growth. Candles and gathered loved ones created moments that still glow in memory.

Tell about a birthday that still brings a smile - the cake, the wishes, the surprises that made your heart flutter.

What birthday cake stands out in your memories?

• Flame glow

• Taste joy

Share about birthday games or activities you loved.

• Friend play

• Joy share

What birthday gifts meant the most to you?

• Most memorable presents

• Why special

Childhood Collections

Some treasures can't be measured in value – seashells from beach days, pressed flowers from garden walks, ticket stubs from special shows. Each item collected held a story and a piece of growing up.

What treasures did you gather and cherish? The precious items that lined your shelves, each with its own special story...

Tell us about your first special collection.

• What you started collecting

• Why you loved these items

Share about where you displayed your treasures.

• How you showed them off

• Where you kept them

What stories hide behind your favorite pieces?

• The story

• Why they're meaningful

First Steps Forward

Each achievement marked a new horizon – first bicycle ride, first lost tooth. These moments built confidence and opened doors to growing independence.

Tell of those moments when you began to find your way – the small victories and the times you surprised yourself and others...

Tell us about overcoming a childhood fear.

• How you faced your fear

• What helped you grow

What moments made your parents especially proud?

• Show shine

• Their reactions

What 'first time' moment changed how you saw yourself?

• The moment

• How it affected you

30

3

Days of Learning and Laughter

Chalk dust and playground memories, friendship bracelets and favorite teachers. Share with us how you grew and discovered your place in the world.

First Day Jitters

New shoes, fresh pencils, and a heart full of butterflies – the first day of school opened a door to a whole new world. Everything felt bigger that day, including the possibilities ahead.

Take me back to that first morning – your backpack filled with fresh supplies, your heart beating with anticipation...

Share about packing your school bag the night before.

• New things

• Care pack

What do you remember about the morning walk or ride?

• Your journey to school

• What you noticed

Tell us about meeting your first teacher.

• First impressions

• How the teacher welcomed you

Classroom Memories

What moments from your school days still make you smile? The chalk dust dancing in sunbeams, the lessons that opened new worlds...

Tell us about your favorite classroom atmosphere.

- How the room felt

- What made it special

What subject first captured your imagination?

- Favorite lesson

- Why it excited you

What classroom moments still make you laugh?

- Funny memories

- Class humor

Favorite Teachers

Some teachers do more than teach - they inspire and believe in us before we believe in ourselves.

Remember that special teacher who saw something in you - their encouraging words, their unique way of teaching, how they helped shape your path.

Tell us about a teacher who believed in you first.

• Faith give

• Heart grow

Share about a teacher's words you still remember.

• Important advice

• Lasting impact

Tell us about a teacher who helped during struggles.

• How the teacher helped

• What you learned

Best Friends Forever

True friendship in childhood is pure magic – sharing secrets, standing up for each other, learning to trust and be trusted.

Who sat beside you through those school year chapters? The shared secrets, and the laughter that got you in trouble...

Tell us about meeting your first best friend at school.

• How you met

• What connected you

What adventures got you both in trouble?

• Mischief together

• Funny moments

Tell us about secrets you shared together.

• Special conversations

• Trust built

Lunch Box Stories

Opening a lunchbox was like unwrapping a daily gift - sometimes trading sandwiches, sharing treats, and creating memories around tables with friends.

What delights did you find in your lunch box? The trades with friends, the conversations, the special treats that made your day...

Tell us about your favorite packed lunch surprise.

• Special treats

• Love in lunch

Share about creative lunch trades with friends.

• Best swaps

• Trading stories

What lunch table conversations do you remember?

• Fun discussions

• Friend moments

After School Activities

When the final bell rang, new adventures began - clubs, teams, and groups where talents were discovered and confidence grew.

What filled your hours after the final bell? Think about the clubs, teams, or groups that added color to your school days.

Tell us about choosing your first after-school activity.

- What you chose

- Why you liked it

Share about a skill you discovered after classes.

- Hidden talents

- New abilities

What team or club felt most like family?

- Group belonging

- Special bonds

Field Trip Adventures

Beyond classroom walls lay exciting discoveries - museums, parks, historic sites. These journeys opened eyes to wider worlds and possibilities.

Where did those yellow buses take you? The excitement of exploring beyond school walls, the new discoveries made...

Tell us about your most memorable field trip.

- Special outing

- Best moments

What discovery amazed you most outside school?

- New learning

- Big surprises

What field trip changed how you saw things?

- Eye-opening moments

- New perspectives

Sports and Games

What activities got your heart racing? The competitions, the teamwork, the victories and defeats that taught life lessons...

Tell us about your favorite PE game or sport.

- Best activities

- Fun memories

Share about team moments that taught you most.

- Learning together

- Team lessons

What victory felt sweetest to achieve?

- Proud moments

- Big wins

School Celebrations

Special events marked the rhythm of school years. Each celebration created memories of community and belonging.

What special events brightened the school calendar? The festivals, parties, and ceremonies that broke the routine...

Tell us about your favorite school festival.

• Special events

• Happy times

Share about preparing for special performances.

• Practice time

• Working together

Share about end-of-year party memories.

• Celebration times

• Goodbye moments

4

Becoming Your Own Person

Wings spread wide, ready to soar. Tell me about finding your voice and those first tastes of independence.

Coming of Age

Every young adult leaves the nest for independence – sometimes in quiet moments of self-reliance, other times through significant challenges or triumphs.

Tell us about the moment you first felt your child truly stepping into adulthood.

Tell us about your first truly adult challenge.

- First big responsibility

- How you handled it

Share about moments that made you feel grown.

- When you felt adult

- Important decisions

Tell us about leaving comfort zones.

- Taking new risks

- Brave changes

Solo Travels

Each journey alone taught lessons about self-reliance, courage, and the joy of discovering new horizons. These adventures shaped both confidence and worldview.

What adventures did you embark on alone? Tell about the places you explored and the confidence you gained.

Tell us about your first solo journey.

- First time alone

- How you managed

Share about unexpected travel challenges.

- Problems faced

- Solutions found

Tell us about memorable local encounters.

- People you met

- Conversations shared

Twenty-Something Dreams

Those years held both uncertainty and unlimited possibility - dreams that seemed both impossible and within reach, hopes that shaped future paths.

What visions did you hold for your future during these years? Remember the goals and aspirations that guided your path.

Share about your five-year plan back then.

• Goals you set

• How plans changed

Tell us about your lifestyle aspirations then.

• Life you wanted

• Dreams pursued

Share about personal growth ambitions.

• Skills you wanted

• Growth goals

First Earned Money

That first paycheck held more than just currency – it represented independence and the sweet taste of earning something entirely your own.

Tell about that initial taste of earning your own money. The responsibility and freedom that came with that first paycheck.

Tell us about your first paycheck moment.

• First earned money

• Proud feelings

What financial lesson hit hardest?

• Money mistakes

• What you learned

Share about work-reward satisfaction.

• Job well done

• Earned pride

Learning to Save

What early wisdom did you gain about managing money? Share the choices between spending and saving that shaped your understanding of value.

What was your first major saving milestone, and how did you achieve it?

- Saving goal reached

- How you succeeded

How did you balance social life expenses with saving goals?

- Smart spending

- Budget choices

Share about your proudest early financial decision.

- Important choice

- Why it mattered

Shopping for Yourself

Standing in stores with your own money brought new freedom and responsibility. Each purchase became a statement of growing independence.

Remember the excitement of making your own purchasing decisions. What items felt most significant when bought with your own money?

Share about a purchase that made you feel truly independent.

• Important buy

• Felt grown up moment

What was the first significant item you bought entirely with your own money?

• Saved up for weeks

• Still remember that feeling

What shopping mistake taught you the most valuable lesson?

• Rushed into purchase

• Lessons learned

Fashion Choices

"Fashion is the armor to survive the reality of everyday life." - *Bill*
Cunningham

How did your personal style evolve during these years? What choices
helped you express who you were becoming?

What was your favorite outfit back then?

• Special clothes

• Why you loved them

Share about a fashion risk you took.

• Bold choice

• Confidence shown

Tell us about your everyday fashion.

• Daily style

• Comfort choices

First Job Stories

Stepping into the professional world brought new challenges. Each day taught something about work and life.

Take us through your entry into the professional world. What surprised you, challenged you, or made you proud?

Tell us about your first job interview experience.

• How you prepared

• What happened

What surprised you most about your first workplace?

• New discoveries

• Real work life

What early mistake taught you an important lesson?

• What went wrong

• What you learned

Professional Style

"Style is knowing who you are, what you want to say, and not giving a damn." - Gore Vidal

How did you develop your workplace presence? Share about finding your professional voice and style.

Tell us about your professional confidence-building moments.

• Challenge faced

• Respect earned

Share about learning workplace communication.

• Speaking up

• Being heard

What professional image adjustments surprised you?

• New adjustments

• Growth shown

Guiding Lights

Every professional journey has its guides. Tell us about the individuals who illuminated your path as you navigated career challenges.

Reflect on the colleagues or leaders who became your advocates in challenging work environments. How did their guidance shape your professional identity?

Tell us about someone who believed in you when you weren't so sure about yourself – how did they help boost your confidence?

• Their support

• Key moment

What's the best career advice you got that might have seemed strange at first but turned out to be really valuable?

• Surprising wisdom

• Lasting impact

What's the toughest feedback someone at work ever gave you that ended up changing how you approach things for the better?

• Hard truth

• Better changes

Values & Principles

Through the journey of building a career, we develop guiding values. Share with us the principles that became your compass in your early professional life.

What core beliefs shaped your approach to work? How did you decide which professional values mattered most to you?

What principles became non-negotiable in your professional life? Tell us about:

· Important values

· Standing firm

How did your professional principles evolve as your career progressed?

· Changed views

· Moments when your values were tested

What helped you stay true to your principles when facing workplace challenges?

· Daily choices

· Strong stance

5

When Love Found You

Hearts recognizing hearts across a crowded room. How did you know? What made you smile? The story of finding your forever love.

First Heartbeats

Everyone remembers that flutter in their stomach. Mom, we'd love to hear about your first experiences with those special feelings.

When did your heart first skip a beat for someone special? Who made you blush and stumble over your words? Tell us about the person who first caught your eye.

Do you remember trying something special to get his attention?

• What gave you the courage

• Whether he even noticed

Was there a moment when everything went hilariously wrong?

• The day it happened

• How you laugh about it now

Looking back, what would you tell your younger self about those early feelings?

• What seemed so important then

• What you understand differently now

Meeting Dad

Some moments change everything - like the ordinary day that became extraordinary when our paths crossed.

Take us to the moment your paths first crossed. What details of that day remain vivid in your memory - the setting and the first impressions?

What caught your attention first about Dad?

• First glance

• Interest sparked

Share about your first conversation.

• Words exchanged

• Laughs shared

Tell us about your first impression.

• Thoughts formed

• Feelings stirred

Special Dates

Each date wrote a new chapter in our story - from simple coffee meetings to elaborate planned outings. Every moment together added color to the canvas of our growing love.

Describe a date that stands out in your memory. What made it memorable, what did you learn about each other that day?

What simple date unexpectedly became unforgettable?

• Unexpected surprise

• Special memory

Tell us about a date where you both couldn't stop laughing.

• What was funny

• How you bonded

Tell us about overcoming a date mishap together.

• What went wrong

• How you fixed it

Letters and Phone Calls

Distance became bridged by written words and late-night conversations. Every letter saved, every call anticipated, wove threads of connection stronger than miles.

Remember the anticipation of each connection, the ways you expressed your growing feelings.

What was your favorite way to stay connected during those days?

• How you connected

• Sweet moments

Tell us about your most memorable phone conversation.

• Stories shared

• Why it mattered

Share about a special letter or note you kept.

• What it said

• Why you saved it

The Proposal Story

> *In that perfect moment, time stood still – hearts beating in sync, future dreams crystallizing into present joy, one question changing everything.*

Bring us into the moment when marriage became your future. What events led to that day, what emotions filled that special time?

Tell us about the exact moment Dad proposed.

• His exact words

• Your reaction

Share about the setting and atmosphere that day.

• Where it happened

• Perfect timing

What thoughts rushed through your mind?

• First feelings

• Happy moments

Wedding Planning Days

"Planning a wedding is like planting a garden of dreams." - Unknown

What memories stand out from preparing for your wedding? Share the decisions and moments that shaped your celebration.

What was the most exciting part of planning your wedding?

• Fun decisions

• Dream details

Tell us about choosing your wedding location.

• Perfect place

• Why you chose it

Share about planning the special details together.

• Important choices

• Working together

Your Wedding Dress

*More than fabric and lace, the dress represented transformation –
from singular to paired, from one story to a shared narrative.*

Tell about finding the perfect dress. What made you know it was the one, how did you feel wearing it on your special day?

Tell us about your dress shopping experience.

- Finding "the one"

- Special moments

What details made your dress special?

- Beautiful details

- Personal meaning

What emotions filled you wearing the dress?

- How you felt

- Dream come true

The Ceremony

Sacred moments filled with promises, surrounded by loved ones, as two paths merged into one shared journey forward.

What moments from your wedding ceremony remain closest to your heart? Share the details that made this milestone uniquely yours.

What feelings rushed through you walking down the aisle?

• Your feelings

• Seeing Dad

Share a special moment with family during the ceremony.

• Family love

• Shared joy

What unexpected moment made your ceremony unique?

• What happened

• Happy memory

First Home Together

Creating our shared space meant blending two lives - finding room for both our stories while writing new chapters together.

Share about creating your first shared space. What touches made it feel like home, what early lessons did you learn about sharing life?

What excited you most about moving in together?

• New beginnings

• Making home

Tell us about your first dinner in your home.

• First meal

• Setting up

What was your first home improvement project?

• What you fixed

• Working together

Early Marriage Days

What discoveries marked your first chapter as a married couple? Tell about adjusting to new routines and building your life together.

What surprised you most about married life?

• New discoveries

• Learning together

Tell us about creating your daily routines.

• Finding rhythm

• Making habits

What early marriage moment made you proudest?

• Achievement together

• Growing closer

Growing Together

How did you nurture your connection through early marriage? Remember the ways you learned to support and understand each other.

What helped strengthen your relationship over time?

• Building trust

• Understanding better

Tell us about overcoming a major challenge together.

• Storm weathered

• Bond strengthened

What discovery about Dad surprised you most?

• New things learned

• Deeper love

6

The Miracle of Motherhood

The profound journey of becoming "Mom." Those sacred moments when you first held us, your heart expanding beyond what you thought possible.

The Happy News

"A baby is something you carry inside you for nine months, in your arms for three years, and in your heart until the day you die." – *Mary Mason*

Share the moment you discovered you were becoming a mother. What feelings rushed through your heart in those first precious moments?

Tell us about discovering you were pregnant.

- First test result

- Emotional reaction

What emotions filled your first moments?

- Initial feelings

- Future dreams

Share how you told Dad the news.

- How you planned it

- His reaction

Preparing the Nest

Every preparation felt sacred – folding tiny clothes, arranging furni-
ture, creating a space filled with love and anticipation for approaching
miracle.

What steps did you take to ready your home for its newest member?
Remember the planning, the organizing, the creating of space.

Tell us about designing the nursery.

• Room planning

• Special touches

Share your favorite shopping experience.

• Important items

• Excited choices

What preparation surprised you most?

• New learnings

• Unexpected tasks

Growing Life Within

Each flutter and kick told stories of the life growing inside - secret conversations between mother and child, a dance of two hearts beating as one.

Tell about the wonder of carrying new life. What moments made this miracle feel most real to you?

Tell us about your first baby movement.

• First kicks

• Special feeling

What cravings surprised you most?

• Food desires

• Funny requests

What moment made it most real?

• Key realization

• Changed feelings

Baby Shower Joy

Surrounded by love and good wishes, celebrating the approaching miracle. Each gift represented not just an item, but the community of support waiting to welcome our little one.

Remember the celebration of your approaching motherhood. What moments from your baby shower still bring warmth to your heart?

Tell us about your favorite shower surprise.

• Special gift

• Happy moment

Share a special message received.

• Kind words

• Touching note

Tell us about the gathering atmosphere.

• Party mood

• Loving support

Birth Story

Take us through the day your child entered the world. What moments stand out in this profound experience?

How did you feel when you first realized your baby was really on the way?

• First signs

• Beginning moments

Paint a picture of those amazing final moments just before our little one arrived.

• Cry heard

• Life changed

When you were bringing this little one into the world, who or what gave you the strength you needed most?

• Who helped

• What worked

First Hello

That sacred moment when we first met - tiny fingers, wondering eyes, perfect in every way. Time stood still as we memorized every detail of this new precious face.

Describe those initial moments with your newborn.

What went through your mind when your baby gripped your finger for the very first time?

- Tiny hand

- Heart melting

Share the sweet story of introducing your baby to Dad and seeing his first reaction.

- His face

- First holds

Paint a picture of that precious first feeding time with your little one.

- Quiet moment

- Close bonding

New Mother Days

What discoveries marked your early journey in motherhood? Tell about finding your way in this new role.

Tell me about a moment in those first weeks when you suddenly felt like 'Yes, I can do this mom thing!'

• Success felt

• Mom pride

What surprised you most about how your life changed in those early days?

• New routine

• Different life

Tell me about finding your own unique way of soothing and caring for your baby.

• Your way

• What worked

7

The Heart of Our Home

Kitchen warmth, bedtime stories, holiday traditions. The beautiful ordinary days that wove our family's tapestry of love.

Home Sweet Home

Creating comfort wasn't about perfect decorations, but about making spaces where everyone felt safe and free to be themselves.

How did you transform our house into a home? Share about creating spaces that comforted and nurtured our family.

What was your favorite room to decorate and why?

• Best room design

• Why you loved it

Which household routine brought everyone together?

• Daily meetup time

• How we connected

Which home improvements made you proud?

• Best changes made

• Great results

Morning Routines

What rhythms did you create to begin our family days? Share the
small rituals that helped us start each morning together.

What was your morning wake-up strategy?

- How you woke us

- Morning system

Which breakfast traditions became family favorites?

- Special recipes

- Morning meals

Which morning chores became natural habits?

- Daily tasks

- Smooth routine

Your Kitchen Stories

The heart of our home beat strongest in the kitchen, where love was measured in cups and spoonfuls.

What recipes became part of our family's story? Tell about the dishes that drew everyone to the kitchen, the meals that became beloved requests.

Share about discovering a recipe that unexpectedly became everyone's favorite.

• Family hit

• Happy cooking

Tell me about learning from kitchen mishaps and turning them into treasured memories.

• Funny mistakes

• Good memories

What creative cooking solutions did you discover during challenging times?

• Innovation sparked

• Problems solved

Family Dinner Tales

Around our table, stories flowed with the passing of plates. These daily gatherings were about more than food - they were about connection, conversation, and belonging.

How did you make our dinner table more than just a place to eat? Remember the conversations and traditions that filled these moments.

Tell me about a memorable dinner conversation that brought unexpected laughter or insight.

• Family stories

• Happy times

What were your creative ways of making weekday meals feel special?

• Simple touches

• Extra care

What kitchen wisdom did you discover that wasn't in any cookbook?

• Smart tricks

• Better cooking

Holiday Traditions

"Traditions touch us, they connect us, and they expand us." - Rita Barreto Craig

What special touches did you bring to our holiday celebrations? Share about creating the customs that made each holiday uniquely ours.

Share about creating holiday decorations that became cherished family treasures.

• Family crafts

• Yearly treasures

What creative touches did you add to make each holiday unique?

• Special adds

• Family style

Share about a holiday tradition you started that took on a life of its own.

• New customs

• Lasting joy

Game Nights

Laughter, competition, and togetherness mixed perfectly on these evenings. Whether winners or losers, we all won at making memories.

What memories stand out from our times of play together? Share about the laughter, competition, and bonding in these moments.

Share about a game night that unexpectedly turned into a treasured memory.

• Fun times

• Happy memories

Share about creating your own unique family games or twisting rules to make games more fun.

• Changed rules

• Better fun

What creative ways did you find to include everyone, despite different ages and interests?

• All ages

• Family unity

Sacred Spaces

Some corners of home held special meaning - the reading nook, the craft table, the garden bench. Places where moments turned into memories.

Which corners of our home held special meaning? Remember the spots where comfort and creativity flourished.

Tell me about creating cozy nooks that became our favorite spots for heart-to-heart talks.

• Talk places

• Close moments

Share about transforming ordinary spaces into magical places for creativity and play.

• Fun corners

• Magic places

What quiet corners did you create for yourself to recharge and find peace?

• Mom's space

• Peace found

Family Gatherings

When extended family gathered, joy multiplied. These occasions wove together different generations, creating tapestries of shared memories.

How did you orchestrate those special times when extended family came together? Tell about creating moments of connection.

Which holiday gathering was most memorable?

• Special celebration

• Best moments

What special dishes always pleased everyone?

• Favorite foods

• Happy eaters

What made reunion preparations easier?

• Smart organizing

• Time savers

Lunch Box Love

Each sandwich made was a message of love. Preparing lunches became a daily ritual of caring sent into the world with our children.

What went into preparing those daily lunch boxes? Tell about the care you took in making each midday meal special.

Which sandwich combinations became favorites?

• Favorite fillings

• Good breads

What special treats did you include?

• Fun snacks

• Extra goodies

Which lunch containers worked best?

• Practical boxes

• Keep-fresh tricks

Bedtime Stories

As day turned to night, stories wove their magic – voices soft, imaginations soaring, creating precious moments between 'once upon a time' and sweet dreams.

How did you transform bedtime into a cherished ritual? Tell about the stories and quiet moments that ended each day.

Which books became regular bedtime favorites?

• Most-read stories

• Why we loved them

Which characters from bedtime stories became household names in our family?

• Family favorites

• Fun names

Which bedtime stories became so special that they're now saved for the next generation?

• Kept books

• Future sharing

Vacation Planning

Each trip, whether big or small, was an opportunity to create shared experiences and stories that would be retold for years to come.

How did you organize family adventures? Remember the preparation and excitement of planning special trips.

Which vacation spot became a family favorite?

• Best location

• Happy memories

Which nature spots captivated the family?

• Outdoor spots

• Family amazement

How did you handle travel emergencies?

• Quick fixes

• Smart solutions

8

Hands That Create

The things that make your eyes light up, your special talents and treasured moments. The pieces of you beyond "Mom."

Your Creative Corner

Creativity flowed through different channels - some days through needle and thread, others through paint and paper. Each project was a way to express love.

Tell about the projects that brought you joy.

Which craft project gave you most satisfaction?

• Best project

• Proud result

How did you find time for creative hobbies?

• Time slots

• Making space

What creative skills improved most?

• Better methods

• Learning path

Garden Memories

What drew you to tend growing things? Share about the satisfaction of nurturing plants and creating beautiful spaces.

What's your most successful garden project or transformation?

· Garden change

· Great outcome

Which plants became your reliable favorites year after year?

· Never-fail growth

· Yearly beauty

How did you learn your most useful gardening skills and tricks?

· Best lessons

· Smart tips

Reading Pleasures

How did you carve out time for reading in your busy life? Remember the books that transported you to other worlds.

What types of books became your go-to choices?

- Loved genres

- Regular reads

When and where did you find your best reading moments during busy days?

- Quiet moments

- Reading spots

Which books surprised you by becoming unexpected favorites?

- Unexpected likes

- New interests

Music in Your Life

What role did music play in your daily routine? Tell about the songs that became soundtracks to different life chapters.

Which songs became regular features in your family routines?

· Daily tunes

· Special moments

How did you discover and collect new music over the years?

· Music sources

· Growing playlist

When and where did you find time to enjoy your favorite music?

· Listening spots

· Perfect times

Movie Magic

Film stories created shared experiences – family movie nights, special outings, favorite scenes quoted. These moments of escape brought us together in laughter and tears.

What films captured your imagination or offered welcome escape? Share about memorable experiences and favorite stories.

What is your favorite movie of all time, and why?

• Best movie

• Special meaning

Which movie scenes or moments particularly resonated with your life?

• Life parallels

• Deep moments

How did you choose which new movies to watch with limited time?

• Choosing films

• Time management

Fitness Journey

"Take care of your body. It's the only place you have to live." - Jim Rohn

How did you maintain your physical well-being? Tell about finding ways to stay active.

What was your favorite type of exercise while raising kids?

- Best workout

- Active choice

When did you usually find time to exercise?

- Workout time

- Daily fit

How did you start your fitness journey?

- First steps

- Early days

Collections & Treasures

Some things spoke to the heart - collected decorations, vintage finds, meaningful mementos. Each piece collected held memories and stories of special moments.

What items caught your eye and heart? Tell about the collections that reflected your interests and personality.

If you could keep just one piece from your collection, which would it be and why?

• Special piece

• Personal value

What's the most interesting story behind any piece in your collection?

• Hidden history

• Fun tale

Which collection piece has traveled the farthest to reach you?

• Long journey

• Where from

Travel Dreams

Whether realized or still planned, travel dreams colored life with possibility – places visited, cultures explored, horizons expanded through wanderlust.

Share about the destinations that called to your spirit.

What's the most memorable place you've ever visited and why?

- Special spot

- Best memory

What's your favorite way to document your travels?

- Memory keeping

- Trip saving

Which destination remains at the top of your travel wish list?

- Wished place

- Future hope

Learning Something New

"Live as if you were to die tomorrow. Learn as if you were to live forever." – Mahatma Gandhi

What skills did you pursue while raising your family? Remember the satisfaction of mastering new abilities.

What new skill or hobby did you most enjoy learning during parenting years?

• New interest

• Fun learning

What's the most practical new skill you learned?

• Practical gain

• Daily help

Which learning experience was surprisingly easier than expected?

• Quick success

• Simple mastery

9

From My Heart to Yours

Your hopes, your wisdom, your dreams for us. The love you wish to pass down, written in your own cherished words.

Building Strength

Difficulties often revealed hidden reserves - teaching resilience, courage, and the power of getting back up after falling.

What experiences built your inner resilience? Share about the challenges that revealed your deeper strength.

What's the most challenging situation that taught you about your own strength?

• Biggest test

• How you overcame

What habit helped you stay strong during tough times?

• Daily strength

• What worked

What's the most practical advice you'd share about handling tough times?

• Real solutions

• Proven help

Marriage Wisdom

Partnership taught that love is both noun and verb - requiring patience, understanding, compromise, and daily choice. Some lessons came easy, others through growth together.

What insights about love emerged through your marriage journey? Remember the discoveries that strengthened your relationship.

What practical daily habits helped keep your marriage running smoothly?

• Everyday acts

• Keeping close

How did you handle disagreements in a healthy way?

• Solving fights

• Making peace

Which communication approach proved most effective?

• Talking well

• Understanding better

Health Discoveries

Wellness became more than physical - understanding the balance of mind, body, and spirit. Self-care wasn't selfish, but necessary for caring for others.

How did you learn to care for your well-being? Share about discovering what your body and spirit needed to thrive.

What daily health habit made the biggest difference in your energy levels?

• Daily boost

• Energy lift

Which stress-relief method worked best for quick recharging?

• Fast calm

• Quick rest

What's your most practical tip for staying healthy on a budget?

• Smart savings

• Healthy choice

Time Management

What helped you navigate the competing demands of life? Tell about finding balance in busy seasons.

What's your most effective method for prioritizing daily tasks?

- Daily planning

- Getting done

How did you handle unexpected schedule disruptions?

- Quick changes

- New plans

What's your best tip for completing tasks efficiently?

- Time saving

- Work smart

Life Lessons

Some truths I learned the hard way, others through joy. My deepest hope is sharing these lessons will light your path and ease your journey.

What essential wisdom do you most want to pass forward? Share the truths you hope will guide your children's paths.

What's the most practical life skill that served you well?

• Best ability

• Daily help

Which decision-making approach proved most reliable?

• Smart choices

• Clear thinking

What's your best advice about choosing life priorities?

• What matters

• Choose well

Living Well

What philosophy has guided your approach to life? Tell about the beliefs that have shaped your path.

How do you define personal success in practical terms?

- Real goals

- True wins

Which life rule or principle has proven most reliable?

- Guiding truth

- Works always

How do you maintain focus on what truly matters?

- Stay on track

- Remember why

Family Values

"Values are like fingerprints. Nobody's are the same, but you leave them all over everything you do." - Elvis Presley

What principles form the foundation of our family? Tell about the values you've worked to instill and protect.

What do you believe is our family's most important core value?

• Heart truth

• Our foundation

Which character traits define our family identity?

• Who we are

• Our strength

What's the most effective way you taught honesty and integrity?

• Truth lessons

• Right ways

Always Remember

Above all else, know this truth: you are loved, completely and for-ever. No distance, no time, no circumstance can change the love in a mother's heart.

What final thoughts of love would you preserve? Tell about the un-changing truths you want your children to carry always.

What's the most important truth you want remembered always?

• Key message

• Remember always

Which life principle should never be forgotten?

• Main guide

• Never forget

What strength do you see that should be recognized?

• Your gift

• True power

Time Capsule

> *Throughout your journey, you'll encounter pivotal moments that shape who you become. I've created these messages to guide you when you need them most. Unlock each one at the right time.*

What insights might your child treasure in these special moments? What truths should follow them through life?

When doubting yourself:

- Trust yourself

- Keep going

During unexpected detours:

- Find good

- Learn new

When celebrating achievements:

- Thank helpers

- Stay humble

My Prayers

Each night, my prayers carried your name, asking for protection, guidance, and blessings on your path. These quiet conversations with heaven were about you.

What blessings have you whispered over your children? Remember the prayers and wishes that filled quiet moments.

Which qualities do you wish would flourish in your children?

· Good traits

· Strong values

Which achievements would bring them lasting satisfaction?

· True success

· Real growth

What life experiences do you hope they'll encounter?

· Important moments

· Growing times

Now Available: Dad's Story Awaits

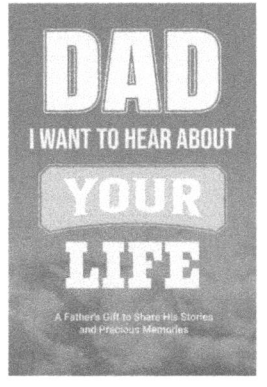

Dad, I Want to Hear About Your Life

Ever wondered what mischief Dad got into as a kid? The moment he knew Mom was "the one"? Those epic fails that turned into life lessons? This book is your ticket to unlocking the adventures and wisdom your father carries. Through perfectly crafted chapters, discover the superhero origin story of your own Dad!

Already capturing Mom's precious memories? Add Dad's volume to create the full picture of your family's journey. (And **Grandparents' editions** to reveal even more family secrets!)

Don't let these stories fade away. Give a gift that grows more precious with time. Because every Dad has a story worth telling.

Available at major online bookstores:

- Amazon

- Barnes & Noble

- and other leading online retailers